Talking to the Bones

Also by Kathy Galloway:

Love Burning Deep (SPCK 1993)
Imagining the Gospels (Triangle 1994)
Struggles to Love (SPCK 1994)
Getting Personal (SPCK 1995)

Talking to the Bones

Poems, Prayers and Meditations

KATHY GALLOWAY

First published in Great Britain 1996
Society for Promoting Christian Knowledge
Holy Trinity Church
Marylebone Road
London NW1 4DU

Biblical quotations from the *Good News Bible* (GNB)
are copyright © American Bible Society 1966, 1976, 1992,
published by
The Bible Societies/HarperCollins Publishers Ltd UK.

British Library Cataloguing-in-Publication Data

A catalogue record of this book is available from
the British Library

ISBN 0-281-04927-0

Typeset by Pioneer Associates, Perthshire
Printed in Great Britain by
The Cromwell Press, Melksham, Wiltshire

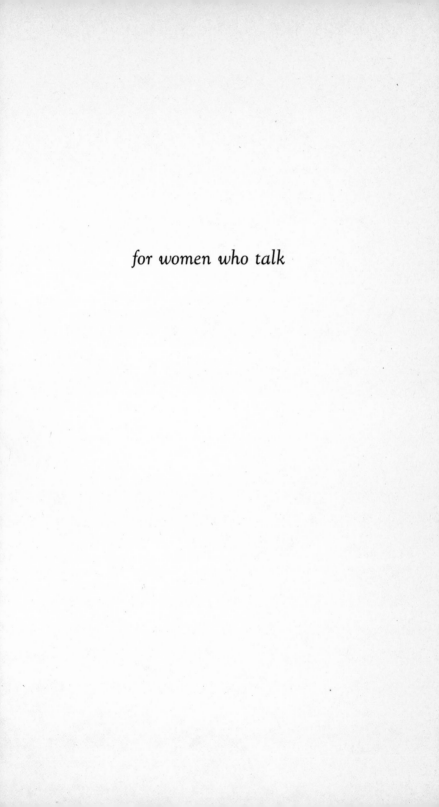

for women who talk

CONTENTS

ACKNOWLEDGEMENTS

I would like to thank a number of people who have supported me, and my writing of different kinds, whose encouragement, friendship and helpful criticism have been invaluable, and, perhaps more importantly, who have continued to love me even when I talk too much.

Thanks to Tom Leonard, Ian Heggie, Jess Kerr, Yvonne Morland, Ruth Burgess, Joyce Gunn Cairns, and many other writers, actors and artists who have been prepared to read, perform and affirm my work in creative ways.

I would like to give particular thanks to my good friend Colin Gray, who has been director, collaborator, critic, and whose encouragement, knowledge and enthusiasm I have appreciated more than I can say.

Thanks to Val Holtom, Penny Stuart and Liz South for much practical and reflective support.

Thanks to my family, especially Lesley Orr Macdonald. It is a source of joy and solidarity to me to have a sister who is also a woman who talks to the bones.

Thanks to my children, David, Duncan and Helen Galloway. In their unique ways, they are all present in everything I write.

Some of these pieces were written when working for BBC Scotland. Thanks to Anne Muir for asking me, and to the people with whom I shared journeys through that work.

Other pieces were first published in 'Coracle', the magazine of the Iona Community. I would like to thank the Glasgow office staff, especially Lesley MacKinnon. I would also like to thank Ron Ferguson, John Harvey and Norman Shanks for their encouragement of my writing.

Thanks also to the editorial staff of SPCK, and to Philip Law, who originally commissioned the book.

There is a long history, inside the church and outside it, of women being silent, and sometimes silenced. Sometimes it has been because what they said was unacceptable, or too challenging or too painful. One of the achievements of the feminist movement has been to recover some of the silenced voices of women from the past, and to make spaces where women today can tell *their* stories. Some of these do not make easy listening. They are stories of abuse, injustice and devaluation. They are survivors' stories. Other women have spoken out courageously against violence and oppression for people who are not allowed to speak for themselves – women like Aung San Suu Kyi of Burma, Hanan Ashrawi from Palestine, and recently, and most tragically, the Irish journalist Veronica Guerin, who was shot dead for her exposure of drugs crime in Dublin. Thank God none of these women stayed silent. For the inspiration and courage of women – survivors, campaigners, artists and writers, theologians, historians, teachers, mothers and sisters and daughters and friends, I am grateful, and therefore this book is dedicated to women who talk.

I felt the powerful presence of the Lord, and his spirit took me and set me down in a valley where the ground was covered with bones. He led me all round the valley, and I could see that there were very many bones and that they were very dry. He said to me, 'Mortal man, can these bones come back to life?'

I replied, 'Sovereign Lord, only you can answer that!'

He said, 'Prophesy to the bones. Tell these dry bones to listen to the word of the Lord. Tell them that I, the Sovereign Lord, am saying to them: I am going to put breath into you and bring you back to life. I will give you sinews and muscles, and cover you with skin. I will put breath into you and bring you back to life. Then you will know that I am the Lord.'

(Ezekiel 37.1–6 Good News Bible)

INTRODUCTION

I have always loved the passage from the book of the prophet Ezekiel in the Hebrew Bible about the man set in the valley of dry bones, and commanded by God to prophesy to the bones, to discover whether the bones can live again.

And lately, it has seemed to me that it is also a powerful metaphor for describing the task of faith as it presents itself anew in every generation and to each person. For all those who find themselves wandering lost in the valley of the shadow of death (whether the death of faith in religious establishments and institutions, or the deaths brought about by betrayal or injustice, or even the death of experienced faith, hope or love), for anyone who looks for help and finds only dry bones, the question comes: *Can these bones live again?* To wrestle with this question is often acutely painful, and always disturbing.

Many of us have come to the point where it is hard to see the bones for the decaying flesh. We cannot live our lives as other than who we are. We are particular, located in a particular history, geography, culture and gender, rooted in relationship. And we are made flesh. In order for faith to live, its bones need to be fleshed with the language, understanding and insights of our lives. We cannot live in, or out of, the faith of the past, or of other places. If we try to do so, we may discover that they are based on mere intellectual assent, or fear-filled security needs, and do not have a solid foundation. They are not dynamic, they are static. They are not personal. They do not live.

Clothing the bones of faith with present flesh happens in relationship. We do not wrestle alone. When God commanded Ezekiel to prophesy to the bones and to the wind, it was the initiation of a most ancient form of learning and discovery: a dialogue of question and answer, of talking and listening and talking back, a dialectic based on the bones of experience, not on the rhetoric of theory. To 'reflect on our experience' can sometimes suggest a rather passive approach. But such reflection is in itself a kind of action, because it takes place in the context of experience. We ask, not the abstract question, *What does this mean?* – a question which belongs in another place – but, *What does this mean for me?* and hence, immediately, *What does this mean for me in my relationships – with other people, with my history and religious tradition, with the scriptures, with creation?* And in asking these questions, we are also asking, *What is my relationship with God? Does it live?*

The conversations of faith that we hold – with others of similar views and those of very different ones, with the scriptures, with the liturgy and doctrine and practice of our churches, with our culture and history and politics, and the conversations of prayer – are ongoing. And they do require a measure of trust, the readiness to undertake a journey with no assurance of what the destination is – or, indeed, without any guarantee of arrival. For this, of course, there is good biblical precedent. As Ezekiel said to the Lord when he was asked if the dry bones could live again, 'Only you can answer that.'

And because of the exposed nature of the journey, there is all the more need for it to take place in the context of relationship, of community. It is fatally easy to exalt one's own subjective experience to the status of a theology, or to confuse one's own needs or self-interest with revealed truth. As well as our own subjectivity, we need the objectivity of others. What seems to be true to our experience must be tested against the experience of others. And even this is relative, conditional. The flesh on the bones will have different forms for different people.

As will the means of exploration. My background and upbringing within the presbyterian tradition have left me with a deep and abiding love for the Bible, its language and literature, its revelation and self-revelation. It comes easily to me to think in biblical themes and images. An ecumenical tendency, nurtured early, has meant a great attachment to the sacramental nature of faith, and a clock which is set to the calendar of the church rather than any other. As a pastor and political activist, I have sometimes found myself on different theological routes from the more familiar ones. And being female in an institution predominantly male in its language, thought-forms, processes and practices is another complicating factor. Though interesting, I have not found it easy to be a catholic presbyterian activist feminist trying to do theology. Sometimes, and most deeply, poetry has seemed the only language available to me.

And though the signposts of my life are those of Christian faith, scripture and church, there have been times when even these have been lost to me, or decayed, times when they needed to die for me, and when I have needed to talk to the bones, to discover whether the bones could come back to life. And for me, many, though not all of them, have. But I think that without such an exploration, they would not have done so.

So, for example, though I begin to see glimmers of how a perception of the transcendence of God may be a possibility for me as someone who, like many, perceives God in immanence, in incarnation, God-with-us, I know I would *never* have arrived at such a point had I remained shackled to the corpse of a transcendence located in a two-tier universe, hierarchical and patriarchal orders, and the censorship and impoverishment of the imagination and spirit that these so often impose. Exploration, openness and the crossing of some difficult barriers, though accompanied by considerable fear and insecurity, have been for me a process of liberation and the renewal of faith.

One of the poem-cycles in this book, *The Road to Iona*, is a reflection on a series of television programmes that I made with the BBC. With a few companions, and also accompanied by an outside broadcast crew, I travelled an old pilgrim route from Glasgow to Iona, encountering places, people and their faith stories and engaging along the way with a number of gospel stories.

Another is a personal interpretation of the Apostles' Creed. This is what it means *for me*.

The *Exodus* poems are the expression of a collective experience and reflection. On Iona in the summer of 1993, a group of about thirty people of different ages, backgrounds and nationalities recognized and named their own experience of exodus in words and phrases. Subsequently I put these in poetic form, incorporating the words and phrases offered by others. For this group of people ancient bones took on new flesh, the flesh of the here and now.

The other poems, prayers and meditations must speak as they will. I do not have the feeling that any of them are definitive, or a last word for me, not as long as I live. This talking to the bones is much too demanding, intriguing and vital a conversation to be abandoned.

KATHY GALLOWAY
GLASGOW

Word and story

EXODUS EXPERIENCE

Home I

There is a place called home.
Warmth and shelter when the wind outside blows cold
    and bitter.
Food for the body and the soul.
Space when I need to shut the door for a while,
lick my wounds, tend my spirit, come back to myself.
Attention, recognition,
                to my needs
                of my achievements.
Things, solid or beautiful or just treasured,
holding memories like fragrant cups,
grounding me firmly in the reassurance
of ordinariness.
And things to do,
tasks that weave the pattern of my days,
for family,
or just for me.
My identity is clear;
a message written out
in tables, pictures, washing on a line,
scattered papers and the smell of coffee.
I am contained, held in safety,
sanctuary.
Here, I am centred.

Home II

But perhaps
there is a place called home,
not spacious but narrow.
Squeezed between the stone of expectations,
generations, family love, familiarity,
and the harder stone of restriction,
limitations and
conformity,
spirits bleed.
Ground between the stones,
sparks of conflict fly,
erupt into violence,
or, ground down,
nostalgia dissipates in boredom
or complacency.
And the stress of unpaid bills
or ironing
goes grinding on.
This does not feel like sanctuary.
Doctrines of security
too often indicate control.
We are edged out
of meaningful participation,
power to choose;
or shoved, face against a wall
that seems too high and thick ever to get over
into the waiting world beyond.

Exile I

Even exile
can feel like home.
Forced out beyond the borders
by threat, oppression,
poverty or unemployment,
the gifts of freedom,
anonymity,
less restriction,
opportunities,
hold a kind of sanctuary.
New perspectives, cultures,
new companions to share bread with
(and bread to share)
allow a re-evaluation
of what has been, is now,
and may be still to come.
And fragile, broken stems
put out fresh shoots,
take root,
nourished by friendship,
choices,
and the choice or chance of teamwork.
For some, awareness grows
of home discovered
or, sometimes, re-created.
Come in from the edge,
the centre is regained,
though shifted to a different place.

Exile II

For some, the journey into exile
is not so happy.
One exclusion exchanged for another,
or oppression just intensified.
Isolation in the midst of crowds.
Alienation sharpened by all the
unquestioning belonging.
Strange languages and even stranger silences
leading to misunderstanding.
Regrets for many kinds of loss
rise up to torment.
And the hunger for identity,
justice,
restitution,
absolution or acceptance
gnaws at vitals and vitality.
There is nothing like a climate of fear
for pushing you to extremity;
to the very edge of known experience.

Desert I

Out beyond the edge of known experience
lies the desert.
Were you driven, protesting all the way?
Were you led, perhaps against your inclination?
Or did you, curiously, choose a way that culture,
church,
or even better logic would have had you leave alone?
In the end it didn't matter.
There you were, across the border,
over the abyss,
taking a long walk off a short cliff.
In this scrubby, hostile wilderness,
there is no shelter, therefore exposure;
no control, therefore vulnerability;
and (worst of all) no signposts, therefore confusion.
Only the stress and strain of hunger
(no ready-made or obvious source of nourishment,
and manna is not sweet like honey),
drought
(this brackish trickle fills a bitter cup),
isolation
(no escape into mirroring others).
And in the dark, fear.
And in the fear, darkness,
fearfully anticipating enemies,
and finding you are actually
facing yourself.
It's not so much being shut out from the centre.
In the featureless desert,
where any step in any direction
holds the risk of your being lost,
there are only edges.

Desert II

You wander the desert for a long time,
a testing-time,
often looking back towards captivity with some regret.
At least there you knew where you were.
Here, you know nothing.
But slowly, imperceptibly,
you stop wandering the desert
and you live the desert.
In solitude and quiet,
you see new things –
the nature of the landscape;
that there are no high-rises blocking out the air;
no structures, strictures,
tramlines, guidelines,
and therefore, many options.
With few possessions, you learn to travel light.
The miracle of survival
and the grace of faith
deepen tenacity,
strengthen determination,
and peace (not as the world gives it)
comes in going on.
A new sense of identity is founded
on the rock beneath the sand, and with no family
    but the family
of the nomads who, crossing your path

more often than you first realized
(now you've got your night sight)
accompany you for a longer (forty years or thereabouts)
or shorter time
Living the desert, it dawns on you
that there are no hard edges, borders, barriers,
only wide horizons.
Everything is immanence.
Everywhere, and nowhere,
is centre.

Promised Land I

You can get very attached to the desert.

Having surrendered, or been abandoned, to
the exploration of lostness,
the element of surprise is always present.
In the land flowing with milk and honey,
will arrival mean disappointment?
Here, there is space for dreams.

Will peace mean boredom?
Here, predictability is never possible.

Will abundance mean complacency?
Here, the shifting sands keep temporary triumphs in
    perspective.

When the promise holds purpose and meaning,
will fulfilment, journey's end, mean loss of meaning?

And worst of all, what if you don't recognize it
when you get there?

But even this attachment must be left behind,
lest it become addiction, or defence.
There is still new learning to be done,
new building to be undertaken,
new freedoms to be entered.

And do you fear your heart's desire?

Perhaps even Jesus left reluctantly,
glimpsing the pain of these new freedoms.

The metaphor fails here,
halted by the politics of conquest, death,
forgetfulness,
and the culture of illusion and exclusion.
Some have gone in and found their true communion,
celebration.
But I think that they have been
only those who bear the marks
of home, exile and desert on their hands and feet
as living memory, even in the promised land,
and suffer them to go on bleeding out of love.
For the rest, the fleetingness of moments
on the mountaintop
are enough to keep alive the longing in us
for the time when there is no division
between the edge in the centre
and the centre in the edge.

Promised Land II

I have read
that when the liberation theologians of South America
studied the exodus story with Christianized Indians,
seeking to help them interpret the scriptures
from their own 'concrete historical reality',
they found it difficult to get the people
to identify with the followers of Yahweh,
'the chosen people',
as might have been expected.
These native peoples,
on the contrary,
found their reality
mirrored in another native people,
the Canaanites,
invaded,
occupied,
their sacred ground trampled,
their convictions mocked,
their promises betrayed,
their history silenced,
their children dispossessed.

How often, it seems,
is the promised land for one
won at the cost of another's
invasion,
occupation,
trampling,
mockery,
betrayal,
silencing,
dispossession.

Is it that there is not enough land to go round?
Or is it that the green land over there,
flowing with milk and honey,
is more desirable
than this barren land,
which would require much labour, hardship,
watering, watching, waiting,
to produce even the smallest shoot?
Well, that is understandable.
If it's there for the taking,
why not take it?
Life is full of injustices,
and the chosen people suffered more than most.

Still, having come to love the desert,
my heart is moved
by that courage which will not see
the promised land
as other than the wilderness
which (that other promise goes)
will blossom,
with resilient, rare
and very beautiful flowers.

TWO WOMEN

The woman with the issue of blood: Shame

Shame, or not shame.
I never know.
I know that all the messages of flesh
and blood scream at me, 'Shame, you should feel shame,
you are not clean, you do not measure up
to what the standard is.'
This seepage, slippage, flow and flood,
this blood that comes and comes
but will not come in proper places
but shames and blames and bleeds
upon the rags of pride and shame
and stains and taints and taunts
and shames and haunts the wretchedness
of those who claim, or would absorb it.
This blood, that I cannot contain,
that rises, swells, torments, distends,
that weakens, wastes, defeats, unsexes,
undermines and unacceptably lays low,
this shame, this means that never finds an end,
this blood, this flood, this torrent never spent,
this shame, this shame, this shame.

And yet,
there is a deeper thing than even blood
that growls within my soul and surges
as the urge of shame is shy to do,
and roars exultant, trembling, fearful of its power.

I WILL TOUCH
I WILL CLAIM
I WILL END

After all,
this too is human,
this too is true.
If human is acceptably
what I am, or you, or you,
then I am this,
and this is human,
and there is no shame
in being this.
And this is, shameless, touching, who I am!

The woman with the issue of blood: You suffered me

You suffered me,
allowed me,
let me touch you,
confirmed me,
authorized my own authority,
permitted me my being,
let me claim that knowledge
which reluctance, fear, or just the shock of boldness
relegated to the silent shadows of my heart,
substantiated it.
Oh, but more,
you honoured it.

You did not turn away, repelled,
condemn or threaten or excuse.
You did not abort, curtail, or clear your throat.
It was not you – I did it, touched you,
made an end to fear, though fearfully I did it.
I am made whole.

I think it cost you – yes, of course it would.
For this I offer no apologies.
Such is the price of love,
for you as well as me.
You paid it with a smile.

I should go, get on,
there is so much to do,
and getting used to living without bleeding
will take some practice.
But I want to spend a few more minutes
savouring the taste of shamelessness
and the fierce delight that lies the other side
of wounded pride.

You suffered me.
I knew you would.
I had faith in you.

Magdalen: The unstated contract

God, give me clean desire.
Give me bold looks and sideways glances,
measured stares and measuring inconsequential words,
the cry of flesh and breath withheld,
the pleasure of the present moment,
something here, and now, and only that.
Something clean.

I am sick of taking to my bed
the endless rehearsed drama of other people's lives.
So much rejected passion, neutered hopes, aborted
    chances,
craven dreams
that never see the light of day
but birth these monstrous and mechanical delusions.
I have played so many walk-on roles,
and spoken umpteen badly written sentimental scripts.
    'Who do you want me to be tonight, darling?
    What is it that you want to feel?
    You want to feel big, I'll do all the necessary
        exaggeration.
    Or how about mean, I can cower with the best.
    I have a splendid line in discipline if that's your bent.
    Or mothering – well, I come highly recommended.
    You want revenge, just take it out on me.'
I am the leading lady in second-hand and third-rate
    fantasy,
I am the well-oiled mechanism to trigger repetition.
All that's required is sufficient imagination to suspend
    reality
for half an hour or so,
and the unstated contract,
'I won't see you, and you won't see me.'

Sex would be a relief if that was all it was.
Give me a sailor with an urge any day.
No past, just present
beats lots of past and just pretence present.

That's my prayer, restore me to appropriate and clean
    desire
before I lose it altogether,
as I have lost the scent of love.

Magdalen: Redeemed

Someone should have told me prayer is granted,
But never in the way you think it should.
So would my heart by lightness quite enchanted
Feel less surprise, though hardly greater good.
This charm of laughter tickles me in ways
And places far removed from those I knew
When prickly lust thrust in my dancing days
Strained innocence away and let guilt through.
The land of innocence is not regained
When once it's lost, but on the farther coast
Its joys, matured, redeemed, may be attained
Even by those who count themselves as lost.
The flow of friendship, trust, this is the tide
That bears us safely to the other side.

THREE MEDITATIONS

The sower and the seed

Autumn is all around me now, beautiful in scarlet and
    gold.
And yet there is a sadness in its beauty.
I know that it means the coming of the long nights of
    winter,
a dark time when the earth seems barren and the trees
    are bare.
And the sadness is also for the darkness in my soul.
There is so much I cannot control, have the way I want
    it to be,
that it feels like many little deaths.

And yet, God is kind.
In the hiddenness and darkness, the seeds of new life
    are taking root,
beginning the long, secret journey to where they break
    through
hard earth, protesting flesh, frozen hearts.
Growth is always painful, stretching, unfamiliar.
But in the dying of autumn, I see the birthing of spring.
God is kind. This is the way of the kingdom.
So I surrender myself to the movement of life,
to the hand of God.

I look at my own hand. It is closed, still clutching for
    what is gone.
But I cannot scatter seed with a clenched fist.
I open my hand. I let go of all that I have been holding
that needs to die.
It hurts to let it go. But it is the hurt of life.
Now I can sow new seed.

My seeds are small. But they have great potential.
I don't know where they will take root.
So I want to sow well, with care;
seeds of friendship and respect, and value for people.
Seeds of justice and love.
Seeds of reverence and encouragement.
I want to sow seeds of peace.

I can only sow.
For the rest, I trust, and I let go.

The final judgement

Once, when I divided the world into goodies
    and baddies,
I always sided with the goodies,
and was full of righteous indignation against
    the baddies.

Later, when the world was less simple,
and I less sure of my own goodness,
I groaned under the burden of perfection,
and feared the weight of judgement.

Now, I have come to know judgement as a teacher.
It has taught me that I am a body that needs cared for.
If one part is neglected, all the other parts suffer too.

And I am part of the body politic –
of a family, a community, a nation,
of the human body
and the earth body.
If one part suffers, all the other parts suffer too.

Misery breeds hostility, hostility, fear;
and fear casts out love.
I am cast out from the body.
This is damnation.

But care gives birth to justice,
justice generates acceptance.
Acceptance is moved to love,
and love overcomes fear.
I am connected to the body.
This is life.

And I no longer groan under the burden of perfection.
I am simply glad to share the sorrows and joys of the body,
and we hold each other up.

So will the nations be judged.

Hungry, homeless, sick, refugee, prisoner . . .

Jesus says, this is my body.

The workers in the vineyard

There's an awful noise in my head.

It's like lines of music all jumbled up,
an orchestra gone wrong.

I try to disentangle them.

I hear the plaintive moan:

> *it's not fair, I've worked hard, in the sun,*
> *all day long, it's not fair*

. . . the shrill whistle of pride:

> *they don't deserve it, they're worth*
> *less than me, less than me*

. . . the trumpet-blast of greed:

> *here's my chance, give me more*
> *give me more*

. . . hardly heard, a faint refrain:

> *but you agreed, this is enough*

. . . and through it all, the dull drumbeat of fear:

> *am I only worth the work I do, the money*
> *that I earn, without that, am I worthless,*
> *redundant?*

The noises jangle on, hurting my head, hurting my soul.
STOP, PLEASE STOP.

Out of silence, a voice speaks.

It's saying . . .

> *the economy of God is different*
> *listen to the ground bass*
> *listen to the bottom line*

I listen, and I hear it, endlessly repeated . . .

> *don't be afraid. Beyond the judgements of the world,*
> *you are precious. You need no value addition.*
> *I am for you.*

I begin to hear differently. The faint refrain becomes a
   silver clarion horn:

> *never less than justice*
> *never less than justice*

And there are grace-notes, dancing, generous:

> *Yes, you too*
> *Yes, you too*

This is the music of the kingdom.
And I don't mind that many will go in before me.
Now, when I am afraid, I will listen for the ground bass,
the bottom line.
And my soul will sing.

PRAYERS FOR A JOURNEY
(Adapted from Psalm 139)

Time to go

Time to go.
Go out,
go home,
go away.
Reluctant or eager,
fearful or full of hope,
it's time to go.

Spirit of the Way,
may we carry with us
. . . oil of kindness for bitter partings
. . . salt of courage for uphill struggles
. . . spice of delight for new surroundings
. . . water of refreshment for parched imaginations
and sweet grace to surrender all we cannot finish
into other hands.

Time to go.

For you are all around me, on every side.
Before me and behind me, your hand is upon me.
And you know my ways and you search me out.

Too much luggage

Oh my Lord,
I am carrying too much luggage,
and it's weighing me down,
holding me back.
I worry about losing it,
but I don't need most of the stuff I'm dragging about.
It blocks up the aisles and gangways,
getting in the way,
making people cross
and wrapping itself round my ankles.
I need to learn to travel light,
but I don't know what to do with all this stuff.

Here,
you take it.
I'm leaving it with you.
Perhaps you can find a better use for it.

For who knows me better than you,
who has given me the substance of my life,
bone and marrow, patterned in my mother's womb?
You are my unfolding and my unburdening.
You are the keeper of my deepest secrets.

When

When I ascend to the mountaintop
and gaze with joy on the other side,
Or when I must travel to places of death;
Cherish my delight, and contain my horror,
For you have been there, and there, before me,
O Jesus of the Way.

And when my journey takes me far across the world
And I must encounter new tongues, new ideas, new ways,
Hold my heart and mind open,
For you are there too, waiting to welcome me,
O Jesus of the Way.

And when my path is black and unlit,
And I can see nothing in front but dark and fearful shapes,
Still my panic enough to know
that one of them is your shape,
O Jesus of the Way.

For where shall I go from your spirit,
And how could I be away from your presence?

If I climb up to the heavens you are there,
and if I make my bed in hell, still you are there.

If I fly east with the rising sun,
or sail to the uttermost west, you are there.

If darkness covers me, and night closes in on me,
you are there too;
for the night is not dark for you, but luminous as the day,
and the two are one to you.

For where shall I go from your spirit?
Your presence is there, and there, and there.

All the saints and angels

I wanted a guardian angel,
to watch over me,
to tell me which way to go,
when I got lost.
But I had to take the risk of travelling
with no guarantees,
And I had to ask for help, and choose between equally
    confusing routes myself.
So, no guardian angel!

On the other hand,
there was that young man who went out of his way
to take me where I was going,
and the girl at the ticket office who spent ages
patiently explaining the connections.
There was the station-master who kept me company on
    the empty platform
when I was waiting for the last train,
and the woman I had a laugh with, because
    she'd left home
with her boyfriend's keys in her bag.
And in the interminable queue for the ferry,
there were the children who sang songs, played 'I-spy',
and gave me cuddles.

For all these saints and angels,
fellow-travellers and guardians of the way,
Giver of the Way, I thank you.

And I will praise you,
for, in my soul I know
how marvellously you have made us.
Your ways are strange,
and full of wonder.

Journey's ending

My journey is near its ending.

O great Giver of the Way,
where I have walked too roughly on the earth,
humble me.
Where I have missed a turning,
redirect me.
Where I have failed to listen, watch or wonder,
wake my senses.
Where I have bypassed, backtracked, or been dead to pain,
break my heart and move me to compassion.

For you are not my small and sketchy map.
You are my ground, and you are holy.
You are the holy ground of refugees and gypsies
of tramps and beggars
of streetsweepers and street-
walkers
of lonely hearts and long exiles
of small steps and great
adventures.
To reverence you, I must reverence them
with justice, grace and generosity.

My journey's end is near.
But you and I go on together.

When I awake tomorrow, I will still be with you.
Searching me out, gazing into my heart.
Watch, lest I follow any paths that grieve you,
and lead me in the way that is everlasting.

Benediction

A blessing on our departures
Without them, we cannot walk the way.

A blessing on our companions
Bread of friendship, bread for the soul.

A blessing on all travellers
Border-crossers, wanderers in strange lands.

A blessing on all the stages on the way
And those who gave us guidance.

A blessing on all those we leave behind
And on their journeys.

A blessing on our lostness and delays
These too are life.

A blessing on our arrivals
Homecomings, new beginnings, bright horizons.

A blessing on the Trinity of journeys.
Giver of the Way, Jesus of the Way, Spirit of the Way.

THE ROAD TO IONA

McCulloch Street

I am travelling in the opposite direction
from where I want to go,
taking the long road round
when I am accustomed to the shortest route,
going the wrong way to get there,
though I am familiar with the right one!

Oh well.
Why not?

The Kingdom is near
(Matthew 2.3)

Here,
among the pots and pans,
Now,
kneaded and rolled into apple pie
fragrant and warm and spicy.
Here,
around the kitchen table,
Now,
present to all the hurts and injustices.

Here,
in the dance,
weaving patterns of conviviality and resistance.
Now,
open house, open hearts.
Here,
listening, respect, encouragement,
Now,
right relationship is not postponed.
Here and now.
Only this.
It is enough.

Millport

Cold wind on a dawn sea.
Warm breath steams up the window
and steaming mugs of coffee warm
cold hands.
Marshmallow ice-cream,
old songs,
tea at the Ritz,
wine and laughter, and,
half-angry, I understand
that I must build in loss.

The call
(Matthew 4.18–22)

Yes, I shall seek to find
what only I can do.
But sometimes 'can'
is only known through 'must'.

Yes, I shall ask to receive
clear directions.
But sometimes all that's left to do
is take the first step
and the next step and the next
because the way ahead is dark
and the map does not go beyond this point.

Yes, I shall knock on the door of certainties.
But it remains resolutely closed.
The only door for which I have the key
is the one on which somebody is hammering
for me to let them in,
perhaps (who knows?) to ask me
to do the thing that only I can do.

Garelochhead

Today we will make a television programme.

People behind cameras and microphones
will begin to be real.
The cracks will start to show.
There will be envoys to Anne,
and Andrew will hop like a pelican.
Small things will change.
Within this gestalt of intimacy
we will eat lasagne,
wander in the magic lands of music,
paintings, poems, prayers,
care for one another,
feel the weight of other people's sadness
and wonder about the true nature of love.
I will travel on a train
feeling like I've jumped ship.
There will be sacramental moments.

But this is good.
I will let go of attachment
to a perfect process, programme, progress,
in order to love what is.

Did I say we were making a television programme?
No.
I see now.
We are on a pilgrimage.

Miracles
(John 2.1–11)

cannot violate the integrity of any other
person, place or thing,
therefore,
cannot interfere with the freedom to be
what is chosen, called out, or created
for good or ill,
therefore,
must tend towards a greater liberation of
profoundest instinct, desire, ability,
whether conscious or unconscious,
therefore,
will honour the intrinsic worth of
every species, form and element,
therefore,
may offer ever-wider possibilities
for greater personhood, decision, and the sacrifice
of a lesser self.

A kind of resurrection, then.

Still, it requires some risk,
exposure, action,
to seek a miracle –
      a new way of seeing
      a new way of standing
      a new way of being
– the risk of finding
everything is miracle –
and so requires the exercise of freedom
in order to respond
in love.

Arrochar: Blessed
(Matthew 5.3)

A layer has been shredded from my skin,
and flakes of flesh float to the ground
in a soft wind of vulnerability.
We are a little raw, a little sore, a little more exposed.
Wounds and weaknesses begin to show their sharper
    lines
below the blurring flood of confluence.
I am more unself-conscious with strangers.
The beginnings of knowledge
are also the beginnings of the long journey
to the place beyond the borders.

My skin being thinner, have I let more in?
I am full, almost to overflowing.
I must go away,
pour out,
become poor again.

I think I am in the right place.
The road onward
and the road inward
have joined.

Auchinellan: Casting out the demons
(Mark 5.1–20)

My daughter dreams of spiders,
shakes with fear, becomes hysterical.
In the daytime, one in her room
has much the same effect as nightmare.
No spider has ever hurt her.
But other things have.
Black, huge, hairy spiders become the carriers
of all her agonies and anxieties.
In my mind, I understand this reasonable explanation.
In my heart, I am distressed to see her so possessed.

Tracy said cheerfully,
'I just take the blame for everything.
It's easier that way.'
She was smiling when she said it.
Other scapegoats in other times in other places
have had harsher sins laid on them
at greater cost.

I watched someone I loved
fall apart before my eyes.
There were times when I could see no sign at all
of the man I thought I knew.
'I have no integrity' he said.
I realized then what disintegration means.

Spiders and scapegoats and falling apart.
Did he hold the people's fears?
Did he carry their sins?
And did the weight crush every form and
    structure in him
for the containment and direction of his passions,
or did he never have them?

He tore apart the chains that bound him,
loosening the furies to rage in all directions,
damaging most of all himself.
There are children like him in our country!

The height of my potential for anger
is the depth of my potential for love.
The height of my potential for fear
is the depth of my potential for courage.
The height of my potential for cruelty
is the depth of my potential for kindness.
The height of my passion
is the depth of my compassion.
That which throws apart, scatters, disintegrates, divides,
hurls in all directions
is the diabolic.
That which gathers together, gleans, integrates, unites,
chooses a path,
is the symbolic.
Cross, ring, book, cup, Word,
these are symbols the diabolic hates.

Sometimes you have to release the diabolic spirits,
let them go in the least destructive way,
loving them as they go.
In different circumstances,
they could have been angels.

Iona Abbey: Breaking the rules
(Luke 13.10–17)

Without a system of formal constraints, there is no creativity. There is only change. (Noam Chomsky)

In the Abbey of Iona
bells ring nine times every day.
When this happens,
attentively,
we cease what we are doing
and proceed to do another thing:
wake, eat, work, pray,
rest, meet, talk, play.
Everything has its place, everything given its due weight.
Every day, sixty or seventy people create the circumstances
in which the bells can ring,
by observing the rules of common life.

Some think that all these bells
must seem loud, intrusive,
regimented even,
allowing for little flexibility
and less spontaneity.
The truth is,
within this system of formal constraints
(which is itself constrained by weather, sea, timetables
and the parameters of a few square miles of rock and sand)
relieved of the considerable burden of
inventing every act of every day anew
and of doing battle with ceaseless yet
repetitive change,
we are liberated for attentiveness,
freed to live the present moment,
and to apprehend the subtleties and nuances
of the task in hand.

Within this solid space
things can be accomplished.
Dreams emerge.
Security builds confidence
to stretch in all directions.
This stretching may, of course,
expand to fill the space
and strain against constraint;
cause argument, dissent,
frustration, fury even.
But this is right and good.
Out at the edges,
on the farthest limits of constraint,
repetition will not satisfy,
destruction will not solve the problem,
avoidance will not mean escape,
stasis is not a realistic option.
One must invent,
create,
wrestle a blessing from the circumstances,
find a way of being both beyond and within the limits.
This is possible (though not inevitable)
more often than you'd think.

It seems that making a television programme
is not so different
from life within the bells.
Different rules, of course.
The same dynamic process.

But
            There are rules for rules!
and first,
the rules must serve the process
not the process the rules,

and second,
when the rules serve the process,
the process, not the rules, will serve the people,

and third,
when the process serves the people,
you will know by its fruits,

and fourth,
when the process is barren,
don't blame the people,
don't change the process,
change the rules,

and fifth,
when the process burns the land,
                    poisons the tree,
                    chokes the bud,
don't blame the process,
don't change the people,
smash the rules,
liberate the process,
release the people.
There is no alternative
to finding new ground,
and making new rules,

and sixth,
there is always a rule,
because there is always a process,

and seventh,
you cannot choose to have no rules,
which simply becomes a process of limitlessness
and has its own internal constraints
which tend towards entropy
and absolute bondage,

and eighth,
you cannot have an end
without a consistent process;
no justice except by justice,
no love except by love,
therefore refer back to the first rule,

and ninth,
the extravagant gesture is the very stuff of creation,
but, without limits, there is no extravagance
in going beyond,
because there is no beyond.

It is also a rule that no rule has the last word.

Last word

. . . and why we taste the bitterness of aching lives
that stretch towards the oil of prayer,
and, joyously, the salt tang of the sea
and the dry tang of wine
with the same tongues,
and why the recognition of a voice from far away
becomes the unimpeded channel for
the unmistakable rush of kinship spirit
and other voices echo seriousness, resolve,
disquiet, concentration, humour and
delectable dispassion,
and why the green land that grows
beauty as effortless as breath
is as wounded in some hidden places
as any body,
and why the unnameable, untameable
white wilderness of the heart
renders up dreams and secrets
more precious than any mountain
in small tremors and an eye for detail,
and why the edge of creation is
only another place of touching the ground,
and why what is not said
matters as much as what is,
and sometimes is anyway,
and why companionship is with bread,
and is bread,
and why . . . and why . . . and why . . .
and how we go on,

are all questions that go beyond
the rules for answers.
The most important thing
is that they are,
and we are,
and they, and we, do.

The last word is always
the one made flesh.

Ceremony and calendar

APOSTLES' CREED

I believe in God . . .

Bpta. Bpta. Bpta!
That's the sound my mouth makes,
puckering like a fish
gasping for words
to express the inexpressible.

As symbols (which is what words are)
power, energy, creativity, life, etc., etc.,
are beyond words inadequate.
As explanation (which is what words are)
procreation, reproduction, etc., etc.,
are as inadequate to describe a process
of which only a part
(and which is never begun or ended)
was when my children broke through my flesh.

But I am not without words.
Without words I am not.
Without words I am out of my element,
a fish groping with mystery.
Let the part stand for the whole
(whatever you call it. For now,
till I find better words,
I will stick with God).
What I believe, propositionally,
is hardly the question, and certainly not the answer.
What I trust,
what I step out on,
that's the thing.

. . . Father Almighty . . .

Well, it's big, isn't it?
That's what it's trying to say.
Dead scary important big guy –
kind, of course,
giving you life, and all that –
but just as likely to take it away at any time
if you step out of line.
That kind of power.
Dead awesome, but still, not remote enough
not to bother you.
In fact, so powerful that it makes it hard to breathe.

My Dad's not like that.
My Dad doesn't mind me being better at some things
    than him.
He likes it.
And he always respects my space.
I like my Dad.

So you can see why it doesn't work for me.
My Dad's the right size for a Dad.
God is something else.
Deep's better for me.
Darkness.
Holding.
Ground.
Always making me be born.
That's what it is for me.

I mean no disrespect
(quite the contrary).
But I don't think that either God
or my Dad
would want me to lie.

. . . *Maker of heaven and earth* . . .

It is a good thing to be a maker.
Breadmaker, pounding breath into dough
on a flat stone;
cake-maker, for celebrations, or chocolate
for times of indulgent misery;
dressmaker, cutting, patterning, fashioning,
fitting to a shape;
toolmaker, the maker's maker;
love-maker, skill-sharing artisan of
pleasure, trust, delight;
baby-maker.

Wood and words, stone and steel,
clay, lace, brick, flower, flour, microchip –
whatever the medium,
it is a good thing to be a maker.
Substantial,
material,
concrete,
the exchange of energies
changing the world.

It's a *great* thing to be a
maker of heaven and earth,
is it not?

. . . and in Jesus Christ, his only Son, our Lord . . .

I have loved this life so much!

When every other passion died
and I walked dead through the days
in a land burnt black with attrition;
only this passion, this life,
dark flame in my darkness,
came to me,
and I, visceral,
naked instinct,
sniffing its heat on the wind,
blindly groped my way towards it,
and it entered me
and it lit me with its darkness
until the land grew green and pale
and every love shone with diamond heart,
a sparkling, shimmering web stretching wide
across the branches of a tree,
and it gave me back my life.

Only this life!

. . . conceived by the Holy Spirit . . .

Wow!

What a brilliant idea!
Who thought this one up?

It's your best one yet.

You ideal lover!

. . . born of the Virgin Mary . . .

Penetrated
in your virgin territory,
not by force
but by desire.

We're all virgin somewhere.

What might *we* birth from that place?

. . . *suffered under Pontius Pilate* . . .

In these non-judgemental days
a lot gets killed
by the washing of hands.

When I come under judgement,
I do not think the scales will be
tipped in my favour
by a basin and towel.

For myself, I have loved those people most
who did not wash their hands of me.
Of my justice
and my injustice.

. . . *was crucified, dead and buried* . . .

not because he was perfect
but because he refused to be divided

not because he was powerful
but because he was free

not because he looked at us
but because we saw ourselves and could not
    bear the sight

not because he was unforgiving
but because we wanted to be justified

not because he was so threatening
but because we were afraid

not because he judged
but because he loved

not because suffering was good
but because keeping faith was necessary

not because of his ends
but because of his means

we do it every day . . .

crucified, dead and buried

. . . *he descended into hell* . . .

. . . and in the darkness, memory,
and in the memory, pain,
and in the pain, the wash of fear,
that, ebbing, carries off all hope,
delight, desire, fulfilment,
courage, confidence and worth,
till there is nothing left –
no thing, no self,
no you, no I,
no past, no present, no future,
only nothingness,
with iron bars of nothingness
more strict than any prison.

'he descended into hell . . .'

who could have believed
there was still one last battle to fight?

. . . on the third day he rose again . . .

What goes up must come down!
A familiar proposition.

What goes down must come up!
is rather more subtle
(though we accept it in the grain).

Three days is a fast trans-formation time
for crossing over from death to life,
sloughing off the wrappings and trappings of the grave.
In the face of such ultimately unimaginable constraints
one can only wonder at the inherent creative power
released in the struggle to love.

. . . he ascended into heaven . . .

a man ahead of his time
and before it
out of his place
and in it
here and there
when and where

a new relationship to time and space
alternative energies

what we don't yet recognize
we give familiar names to!

... and is seated at the right hand of God ...

Where's that?
Right from what angle?
Why sitting?

The language of the royal court.
But the royal court is, to me, a theatre.
So perhaps, an actor turned director,
interpreter of story,
lover of the play,
close to the author's mind,
encourager of many outcomes,
improvisings,
explorations.
Yet always attentive to the inner structure,
rhythm,
stretching forms,
allowing creativity;
respectful of the actors, and,
though clear about their shortcomings,
responsive to requests for help.

Yes.
This has meaning for me.
This I can trust.

. . . from thence he shall come to judge the living and the dead . . .

judgement, be my friend.

I am stripped bare.
I have reached the end of the road of
running away.
It didn't get me so far that I could
get away from myself.
Now, I have nothing to cover my nakedness,
nothing to eat but my words,
only myself for company
and the conversation keeps drying up.

a good friend doesn't let you get away with murder
but will speak for you in your defence

a good friend asks hard questions
but stays with you while you struggle with the answers

a good friend sees you at your worst
but still loves you

a good friend has had plenty of practice
in forgiving you

a good friend has no illusions about you
(knows you're only human)
but still has hopes for you

everyone needs a good friend,
otherwise you'd just go on making the
same old dreary mistakes

judgement, be my friend.

. . . I believe in the Holy Spirit . . .

. like the way I feel towards people, listening to Van
  Morrison, warm and mellow
. like the moment of openness just before creativity surges
. like the gestalt of a good letter
. like the tiredness after a day's hard work
. like sudden attentiveness to a tree
. like being stirred by a woman's courage
. like being touched by a man's tenderness
. like the passionate apprehension of a justice
  or an injustice
. like the sure conviction of love
. like . . .
. like . . .
. like . . .

   everything that flows
   everything that yearns
   everything that sings like a steady current
   everything that makes the connection
   pulling me deeper into the solitude of God
   drawing me out into the community of God

   in, out

   in, out

   breathing me

. . . the holy Catholic Church . . .

It's only holy if everyone is in it.
It's only holy if it's whole,
even in all its broken-ness:
catholic in its tastes
protestant towards its certainties
orthodox
unorthodox
all are necessary:
none can be dispensed with.

None *are* dispensed with.
This is an important thing to remember.

. . . the communion of saints . . .

I used to scatter ashes of people on the green land of
    Iona
and sometimes the whirling wind, altering direction
would blow them back on me, and dust clung to my
    clothes,
my skin, my hair.
But I did not mind.
Their dust is mine, and mine theirs.
I, we, they, all of us,
partake of one another's dust,
change,
exchange,
are incorporated.

And my grandmother,
and William Shakespeare,

and Brian, lying near John Smith on Iona,
and John Smith too,
and Columba, and the black slave saint who said,
ain't I a woman
and the man who said, *this time together*
will always be a part of me,
and the woman who is where I am not for me,
and I for her,
and children and women and men
are all a part of me
and I of them,
incorporated,
in communion,
speaking, moving, living
in each other,
breathing in each other
on and on and on.

I give great thanks.

. . . *the forgiveness of sins* . . .

Not thought.
Its logic is remorselessly impotent.

Not feeling.
There are too many of them in an hour.

Not wish.
My desire eats itself.

Not instinct.
It locks into my bones.

Only action.

After an action, everything is changed,
including me.
After an action, there is movement.
Thought, feeling, will, instinct, are different,
even if only a little.
The ground has shifted.

Now,
what is the necessary action?

. . . *the resurrection of the body* . . .

suffering when one part suffers
feeling the pain
not denying or suppressing
not indulging or inflicting
attending to,
tending
or just bearing
till healing comes.

delighting when one part delights
appreciating, applauding
giving a cheer
tingling with anticipation
shiveringly melting with enjoyment
tasting the pleasure
stretching to fill the space
curling into rest.

justice in every part
joy in every part
in every part, fully alive

. . . *and the life everlasting*

The light
from the bright star I am following
left it a billion years ago.
Yes.
This.

Kathryn gave birth to Helen . . .
Janet gave birth to Kathryn . . .
Sarah gave birth to Janet . . .
back towards the star,
onwards to the star.
Yes.
This too.

I held a child in my arms.
You cried for me.
We spoke without words.
You knew me.
The people sang.
A leaf fell.
Yes.
This too.

The knowledge of love.
The star of God holds.

SACRAMENT

Sacrament I

In the train,
a beautiful young man in a green jersey,
dark-haired, white-skinned, red-lipped,
ate glowing scarlet strawberries
with an air of dreamy abstraction.
Enraptured,
savouring this feast of flesh and fruit,
I am in communion with everyone
(lovers, artists, sticky-mouthed children,
ripe girls, men black with dust and dry of throat,
old ladies with cut-glass dishes,
travellers on hidden lanes)
who has ever delighted
in the graceful
taste of strawberries
and beautiful young men
and the word made flesh.

Sacrament II

I have sat here many times
watching the breaking of bread
and the raising of the cup,
and felt many things.
Anger at exclusion,
shame at division,
incomprehension at abstraction,
sadness at separation,
frustration at a beautiful simplicity
tangled into twists of dogma.

But this is gift.
It is a sacramental moment.
This is, after all,
the sacrament of brokenness.

Bread is not broken to be stuck back together.
Life is not broken to be stuck back together.
Wine is not poured out to be put back in the bottle.
Life is not poured out to be put back in the bottle.

We incorporate brokenness into ourselves
and are made whole.
This absence is an appropriate remembering.
I am nourished by my empty-handedness,
refreshed by my dry throat.
These, more than the other, will ensure
that I will sit at dinner with my children,
in a cafe with a friend,
in a bar with strangers
and it will all be remembering
and it will all be sacrament.

Eucharist

Lord Jesus,

thank you for inviting us to your table
for here, you show us our lives

> the daily bread of our work and care
> the wine of delight, pressed from the fruits
> of our creativity
> and our brokenness, with all its pain
> and appalled self-knowledge

We celebrate the life that is ours
for your eternal word is
that it is precious in your sight

And here you offer us your life

> broken to share life
> poured out to renew life
> promised to transform life

We celebrate the life that is yours
pattern of reality for us

And here, your life and our lives
become one in spirit and in flesh
moving out into the life of the world

We celebrate the life that is love revealed

> love given and received
> love in action.

O taste and see

Now is the time for the good wine
Pressed from the fruit of the tree
Now is the time for rejoicing
In the place where the feast will be
O taste and see
And refresh us with love.

Leave all the cares of the growing
Just let the mystery sing
Magic of ripening and pruning
And the fullness that time will bring
O taste and see
And refresh us with love.

Sweet-tasting cup of our loving
Promise of pleasure and pain
Take it and drink of it deeply
For the new life it will contain
O taste and see
And refresh us with love.

(Tune: Frankie and Johnny)

Offering

Lord Christ,

help us to have the courage and humility to name our
    burdens
and lay them down
so that we are light to walk across the water
to where you beckon us.

Our pride,
armouring us,
hardening us,
making us defend our dignity by belittling others –
we name it
and we lay it down.

The memory of hurts and insults,
driving us to lash out,
to strike back –
we name it
and we lay it down.

Our antagonism against those
whose actions, differences, presence,
threaten our comfort or security –
we name it
and we lay it down.

Our fear,
of unsolved questions,
of the unknown,
of fear itself –
we name it
and we lay it down.

We do not need these burdens,
but we have grown used to carrying them,
have forgotten what it is like to be light.

Beckon us to lightness of being,
for you show us it is not unbearable.
Only so can we close the distance
Only so can we walk upon the water.

It is so.

Blessed are you, Lord Christ, who makes heavy burdens
light.

Amen.

PRAYERS FOR CHRISTMASTIDE

No room: An approach

The door is closed. There is no room.
Our Brother Christ is born outside the inn.
O God our life,
you found yourself excluded, crowded out,
out to the edge of life,
where folk who do not have the powerful passwords
    that open doors
struggle to make do with almost nothing,
and yet bear love and hope amid the straw.
And as we, misguided, seek you where we'd like to
    find you,
open our eyes to the star that still shines to lead us
out of our comfortable churches
out of our circles of contentment
out beyond the closed doors of our hearts
to the darkness where the star will come to rest.
And there,
where people feel themselves redundant to requirements
                            unwanted at the party
                            left out in the cold
we will find you, bearing love
making your centre at the edge
room where there is no room.

Birth: A confession and invocation

O God, Creator Spirit,
you pierce us with the joy and pain of birth.
In your embrace we have found potential for new life,
in your wisdom, we have waited for the time,
and now you place your insistent demand upon us.
In us, your Word will be made flesh anew.
And so we pray for your presence and for our
    deliverance.

From dulling our senses against the joyous beauty of
    creation
From numbing our sensitivity against earth's cries of
    pain
GOOD LORD, DELIVER US

From accepting the illusion that tries to sell joy
From judging the painful longing that tries to buy it
GOOD LORD, DELIVER US

From deadening the joyful energy of giving birth
From refusing the painful loss of control of allowing
    birth
GOOD LORD, DELIVER US

From denying the joy of being cherished
From fearing the pain of being stretched
GOOD LORD, DELIVER US

From forbidding others to share our joy
From forcing others to bear our pain
GOOD LORD, DELIVER US

O God, Creator Spirit, you took flesh to hallow all our
    births.
As our sister Mary laboured
As our brother Joseph served

As our brother Jesus was born to realize the Word of
love,
deliver us to be your new creation
and sharers of your creativity
so love may live in us, and we in love.
So we pray in Jesus' name.

Angels and shepherds: A proclamation

Now is the time to put down our cares
        to lay aside fears
        to get out of the rut
Now is the time to hurry to Bethlehem
        to listen to angels
        to trust in a mystery
WITH ANGELS AND SHEPHERDS, HEAVEN AND
   EARTH
SING GLORY TO GOD AND PEACE
   TO THE WORLD

Here is the place where dullness is brightened
        where guilt is forgotten
        where weariness lifts
Here in this place, familiar or foreign
        dreaded or dear
        heaven breaks in
WITH ANGELS AND SHEPHERDS, HEAVEN AND
   EARTH
SING GLORY TO GOD AND PEACE
   TO THE WORLD

These are the folk, kids with bright faces
        and doting grandparents
        friends and relations and people next
        door
These are the folk, strangers, outsiders, passed in the street
        hurting or happy, threatening or kind
        all of them named in the language of
        love
WITH ANGELS AND SHEPHERDS, HEAVEN AND
   EARTH
SING GLORY TO GOD AND PEACE
   TO THE WORLD

Ours are the bodies, growing or ageing
                    broken or bleeding
                    this is the flesh your love took to
                    heart
Ours are the bodies called to live as we bless
                         to act as we sing
                         to step out on the Word
WITH ANGELS AND SHEPHERDS, HEAVEN AND
    EARTH
SING GLORY TO GOD AND PEACE
    TO THE WORLD

The killing of the children:
A litany of intercession

A sound is heard in Ramah
the sound of bitter weeping.
Rachel is crying for her children;
she refuses to be comforted,
for they are dead.

. . . pray for the holy innocents of Israel
Lord have mercy upon us, Christ have mercy upon us

. . . a sound is heard in Gaza, the sound of bitter
weeping
pray for the holy innocents of Palestine
Lord have mercy upon us, Christ have mercy upon us

. . . a sound is heard in Sarajevo, the sound of bitter
weeping
pray for the holy innocents of Bosnia, Croatia, Serbia
Lord have mercy upon us, Christ have mercy upon us

. . . a sound is heard in Goma, the sound of bitter
weeping
pray for the holy innocents of Rwanda
Lord have mercy upon us, Christ have mercy upon us

(intercessions may be added as appropriate, finishing as below)

. . . a sound is heard in our land, the sound of bitter
weeping
pray for the holy innocents in our midst
Lord have mercy upon us, Christ have mercy upon us

They brought gifts: A thanksgiving

Gold

Like the morning on the wing draws the dawn across
    the day
Like the glow upon the faces of children at play
Like the splendour of the love held within the lover's eyes
Are the rare and shining moments that brighten our lives
They sparkle and dance, then grow pale and fade away
But we hold them in our hearts and they warm a colder
    day
And give thanks for their gift and the promise they say
Of the chance to be surprised by the glory in the grey

Frankincense

In the sweet familiar round of ordinary things
In the quiet reassurance that carefulness brings
In the blessing of the bread and the friendships that we
    share
In the everyday obedience of just being there
There is grace beyond measure and charm beyond compare
We are served in every moment by someone else's care
Oh give thanks for the life and the wisdom to say
We have power to discover the glory in the grey

Myrrh

When the shadows close around and we stumble on our
    way
And the ashes of our dreams grow cold and grey
When the broken bread of life is bitter to the taste
And the ground on which we stand becomes a barren
    waste

In these moments of death, something new is coming to
   birth
And the rose of love grows strongest upon the blackest
   earth
Oh give thanks for the love and the freedom to say
We are sharers in creating the glory in the grey

Naming and presentation:
A dedication

God of many names,
my name is known to you.
I am held in the hand of your life,
and I do not know what you will make of me.
All I know is that I cannot make myself
any more than I could in my mother's womb.
But this I can do,
this I choose.
To give myself into the hand of your continuing
    creativity;
my past, with its joys and triumphs, its failures and
    regrets;
my present, with its struggles and accomplishments, its
    hopes and setbacks;
my future, with its fears and freedom, its pain and
    promise.
To loose and to bind,
to stretch and to shape,
to become what I will,
trusting the hand that made the world
trusting the spirit that breathes life
trusting the love that will not let me go
trusting the promise of the Word made flesh.

Flight into Egypt: A benediction

Our brother Jesus,
you set our feet upon the way
and sometimes where you lead
we do not like or understand.

- bless us with courage where the way is fraught with
    dread
- bless us with graceful meetings where the way is
    lonely
- bless us with good companions where the way
    demands a common path
- bless us with night vision when we travel in the dark
                keen hearing where we have not sight
- bless us with humour – we cannot travel lightly
    weighed down by gravity
- bless us with humility to learn from those around us
- bless us with decisiveness where we must move with
    speed
- bless us with lazy moments, to stretch and rest and
    savour
- bless us with love, given and received
- and bless us with your presence, even when we know
    it in your absence

lead us into exile
until we find that on the road
is where you are
and where you are is going home.

Bless us, lead us, love us
bring us home
bearing the gospel of life.

EASTER

An Easter prayer

Christ our life,
you are alive in the beauty of the earth
   in the rhythm of the seasons
   in the mystery of time and space
   ALLELUIA

Christ our life,
you are alive in the tenderness of touch
   in the heartbeat of intimacy
   in the insights of solitude
   ALLELUIA

Christ our life,
you are alive in the creative possibility
   of the dullest conversation
   the dreariest task
   the most threatening event
   ALLELUIA

Christ our life,
you are alive to offer re-creation
   to every unhealed hurt
   to every deadened place
   to every damaged heart
   ALLELUIA

You set before us a great choice.
Therefore we choose life.
The dance of resurrection soars and surges
through the whole creation.
It sets gifts of bread and wine upon our table.
This is grace, dying we live.
So let us live.

HOLY AND ONE
HOLY IN POWER
HOLY IN ENERGY
GLORY TO YOU
          GLORIOUS THE HEAVEN
          SACRED THE EARTH
          FULL OF YOUR CLARITY
          GLORY TO YOU
                    BLESSED THE ONE
                    COME IN YOUR NAME
                    HIGHEST HOSANNA
                    GLORY TO YOU

Christ our life,
in broken bread and poured-out wine
we remember that the love which suffers
is the love which saves.
But your word to us is that it is the love which saves
and not the suffering.

So we say *no* to hunger, homelessness and squalor
    we say *no* to racism, cruelty and economic injustice
    we say *no* to warfare, ethnic cleansing and the fouling of
        the earth
    we say *no* to sexual abuse, misuse of power and the
        manipulation of desire
    we say *no* to misery, fear and frozen hearts
    we say *no* to division, pride and closed minds
No in our politics, in our economics, in our cultures.
Not because we are good, but because we love.
Because we love, we say *no* to glorifying pain.
The glory of the cross is not the suffering but the love.

Looking in the wrong places

Lord Jesus,
we are always looking for you in the wrong places;
among the good and respectable people,
when we should know you are to be found
with the poor and disreputable and outcast.

Lord Jesus,
we are always looking for you in the wrong places,
at a safe distance,
but you come so close to us,
nearer to us than breathing.

We look for you in churchy things,
but we are more likely to find you
among the pots and pans,
or around the kitchen table . . .

We look for you in buildings,
but you walked crowded streets,
and shorelines
and mountains . . .

Even now, even after Easter,
still we insist on trying to find you among the tombstones;
among long-dead dogmas,
in old, decaying fears and hurts,
in the guilts and resentments we inhabit like a coffin.

But the angel said:
Why do you look for him among the dead?
He is not here!

Lord Jesus, help us to lay down the graveclothes,
roll away the stone
and come out into life,
here and now.

We will find you,
among the living,
ahead of us, going to the Galilee we seek.
You have wrestled death to the ground,
and now there is nowhere we can go,
no darkness we can enter,
which is not God-encompassed.

Clinging to the cross

When you're in the sea
and it's very dark
and very stormy
and very cold
and actually you think you're drowning
and you're very scared
and you see a piece of wood
drifting by in the middle distance
you don't hang around to ask questions
or to speculate about how it got there
and why
and who sent it.
You just swim as hard as you can towards it
and you grab it
and cling on for dear life.

In the back of your mind you know
it's not a boat
and it will not give you
either direction
or control.
You're still at the mercy of the flood tide
and whether you like it or not
you're going where it takes you.
But to be honest
you don't care.
You just want not to drown
and the wood offers hope
support
a bit of respite for your aching arms and back
a feeling of not being completely abandoned
something solid to hold on to in the

midst of all this insubstantial water and dark and wind
and stop you panicking.
A way to give yourself up to the sea.

I haven't reached dry land yet
but I'm in sight of the shore.
The piece of wood is still with me
and it's funny
but I've got to kind of like being
in the water.

Of course, it's easier to say that
when you can see land!

STAGES OF LIFE:
THREE MEDITATIONS

A time for birth

A time for birth.
Yet so much of birth is waiting:
a seed planted in dark earth, slowly taking root;
an idea, moment of inspiration, slowly taking shape;
a talent, hardly guessed at, slowly unfolding;
a love, scarcely noticed, slowly maturing;
a child, original creation, slowly forming.
So much of birth is waiting, in darkness.
It cannot be hurried, this time for birth.

And then, suddenly, I am outraged by pain,
tearing my flesh, tearing my soul,
battering at all my resistances,
pulling down all my defences.

I must embrace this?
I had not thought co-operation with life's rhythms
would hurt so much.

Nothing ever turns out the way you imagine,
but slowly, painfully, I am learning to trust
the wisdom of birth.

In the darkness of waiting, God was.
And I see now, it was good.

In the new life being born, God was.
And I see now, it was good.

In giving birth, I see that I too am changed,
a new creation,
and it is good.

The wisdom of birth is God's gift to me,
and my gift to the world.

I give great thanks.

This love will carry

Oh, the adventure of it!
Playing at being grown-up,
keeping house,
unable to keep your hands off one another,
always wanting to touch, to fight, to hold.
Wondering at the mystery of this beloved stranger,
not noticing the days slipping by,
and the strangeness becoming comfortable.

And love, like a scarlet ribbon,
winding its way in and out of
the sweet, familiar round of ordinary things.
This love will carry.

Walking silently by your side
when you're too choked for words.
Getting you through the bad days
with a mixture of sympathy and straight talking.
Being a place to run for cover,
and sometimes,
a boot up the backside.
Taking the first step to close the distance between you,
and, when you're dying of failure,
helping you believe that you're not as worthless as you feel.
Not at all.
This love will carry.

Respectful,
feeling for when to speak and when to keep silent.
Appreciative,
enjoying your differences as much as your sameness.
Relaxed,
not worried any more about seeming foolish.

Being yourself,
because trust is there.

And love is a sea,
taking you to undiscovered lands.
Finally,
you are in your element.
This love will carry.

'You were here, and now you are not'

There is nothing to compare with the pain of death.
You were here, and now you are not.
That's all.

I search for you in old photographs, letters,
things you touched,
things that remind me of you,
but they cannot fill the space you occupied.

The space is in me too,
bleeding round the edges where you were torn away.
In the night, strange shapes haunt the space . . .
regret, fear, fury,
all the things we might have done,
all the shattered dreams.

How can I go on with this hole inside me?
Partial person!
Don't let me fill the space with the wrong things.
Don't let me cover it up,
to eat me from within.
Give me courage to bear my emptiness,
to hold it gently
till the edges stop bleeding;
till the darkness becomes friendly;
till I see the star at its heart;
till it becomes a fertile space,
growing new life within it.

If I had not loved, I would not have wept.
This love you have given me;
this love I have carried;
this love has carried me.

And I know that though I cannot see you, touch you,
the love does not go away.
Carried by this love,
we are not divided.
And there will be no more weeping.

The other self

Marked man

He bears the marks of suffering
on his flesh and on his soul.

The white-hot fire that leaps and soars,
roaring like a lion through steamy jungles
and dark, long-walled ravines,
emerald-eyed and glittering;
or flickers delicately, casting dreams and shadows
in tall pillars ascending to blue heavens;
this fire chars and crumbles
smoking, scorching,
choking into barren blackness,
empty night.

A cold starlight glimmers.
A peal of bells sings out across green land.
A spring of running water mirrors flame.

He carries woundedness precisely,
neither denying
nor idolizing,
only recognizing.

To me, he is beautiful.
He is who he is.
To me he is beautiful.

Skeleton woman

What's that noise?
I don't recognize it.
I am afraid of it.

Did he say something that made you embarrassed for him,
reveal some ignorance, intolerance, lack of character?
Did you think, 'I would be ashamed of him,
in company, with friends, with the people who matter'?
He's not what you thought, is he?
You're evaluating, weighing up, reconsidering.
That noise, drowning out the old accustomed sounds!
Listen carefully.
It's the rattle of bones.

Something moved there!
I swear I caught it,
but I don't know what it was.
I don't like it.

You're not comfortable with that woman, are you?
She moved in too close,
kicked your tender soul around the room a bit.
She was ugly in a certain light,
and her need is so naked (though she thinks it
    well-concealed)
that it leaves you with that most unpleasant feeling
of resentful and exasperated pity.
See that movement?
Watch out.
There's a carcass dragging itself across the ground
towards you.

I saw something gleam in the dark.
It's not a friendly light!

The fear behind the mask, panic beneath bravado,
you scratched and you knew it was there,
and the knowledge was not what you wanted.
You wanted confidence, strength,
a lean and muscular sureness
that placed every step correctly,
not the hungry child in the adult,
not the wounds of the parent,
not the unattractiveness of the lover,
not the frailty of flesh,
bitten nails, stretched skin, falling hair
and the craven backward glance.
Whistle in the dark!
What you see is a skinless skull
and a toothless jawbone clicking
and white bones jerking.

It's so cold in here.
In my chest.

Feelings turn, and fire gives way to ice.
You draw back, move away, perhaps you run.
The creeping paralysis of mind and heart
are only matched by nauseous weariness
that turns the stomach.
No spark, no warmth, no hope,
the coffin-cold of death invades your nostrils,
chokes your life,
chills the marrow and the blood.

Who is she?
She's skeleton woman.
Who is she?
She's lady death, from whom you flee.
Who is she?
She's all of them.

Who is she?
Look in the mirror.

You must
talk to the bones,
hold the carcass to your heart,
stroke the skull and kiss the toothless lips,
caress the jerking bones,
breathe into the coffin-mouth.
If you love your life,
give her flesh.
Then her sinews will knit together,
muscle will stretch, blood flow free,
heart pump, and she will breathe,
and live, and rise, and smile,
and make love to you
all night long.

Skeleton woman.
Your lover.
Your hope.
Your joy.
Your life.

Outside holiness

I expect that the prostitutes Jesus mixed with
looked a lot like Audrey Hepburn, beautiful and
fragile and fallen,
and nothing like the fifteen-year-olds on crack cocaine
down Anderston way,
who'll do anything you like (including risk AIDS)
for a tenner.

And I daresay the publicans cleaned up their language
along with their profits
when they drank wine with him,
and none of them would ever have a hangover
the next day.

Probably the tax-collectors were amenable to
rescheduling debt repayments
(it's a dirty job, but someone has to do it)
and never smashed up furniture
or fingers
when people got behind.

I'm sure carpenters then never told dirty jokes,
housewives never screamed at their children
(or worse, their men)
and no one *ever* said the Palestinian equivalent of
'fuck'.

The man possessed by demons
couldn't possibly have been a schizophrenic
taking his chances with care in the community,
fishermen couldn't have been politicized
and thirteen-year-old boys didn't read
The Acid House,
but instead could be found in churches
when they did a runner.

All of which is a shame,
because I'd like to think that Jesus
has a place in the world I live in.

Of course, I could be wrong.

Rejoicing in heaven

She sings like a raucous angel.
The Blessed Patsy Cline of Pollokshields;
and heaven applauds.
Earth, on the other hand,
whose taste is in its arse,
has not been so appreciative,
and has rewarded her with
abusive men,
crummy houses,
rotten jobs
and a tendency to badmouth her
when she drinks too much.
However, I have it on good authority
that when Celia sings
saints start swaying their hips
and archangels go all dreamy.
They like a bit of attitude in heaven.

Prayers of the veil

In many countries, women wear the veil as a sign of identity, as a sign of self-worth, as a mark of integrity. But it is not always so.

Hidden and mysterious God,
we seek you in darkness and unknowing,
and you come to us with tender love.

We pray for: women who suffer because what should be
uncovered is covered up . . .
women who have been abused as children
and dare not tell . . .
women who have been beaten, tortured,
threatened, and cannot tell . . .
women who have been humiliated, harassed
and terrified, and are ashamed to tell . . .

forgive us, and your church, our complicity in silence and concealment.

Lead us into your liberating judgement, and come to all women who feel powerless, ashamed and fearful, calling them by name, raising them up to stand in the glorious light of your justice and freedom.

For nothing can be hidden from you: everything in all creation is exposed, and lies open before your eyes. (Hebrews 4.13 GNB)

In many countries, women wear the veil when they marry, as a sign of covenant and rejoicing. But it is not always so.

Beloved God,
in desire and intimacy you come to us,
and know us as a lover.

We pray for: women whose bodies have been violated by
            rape, sexual torture and the slow drip
            of degradation . . .
          women whose bodies are bought and sold as
            commodities, in prostitution, in porno-
            graphy, in sex tourism . . .
          women whose cultures reflect them as
            inferior, as stereotype, as valuable only in
            certain roles . . .

forgive us, and your church, our failure to proclaim the true
personhood of all people, regardless of race or gender.

    Lead us to see others with the eyes of Christ, and touch
all women who have learned to hate, punish or mistrust
their own bodies with the dignity of those made in the
image of God.

*How beautiful you are, my love! How your eyes shine with love
behind your veil. (Song of Songs 4.1 GNB)*

*When women give birth, the veil of flesh covering the womb is
torn, so that new life may come with hope and delight. But it is
not always so.*

God of power and presence,
midwife of our lives,
you encourage and calm us into creativity.

We pray for: women forced by desperation into back-street
            abortion . . .
          women who must give birth in dangerous or
            squalid conditions . . .
          women who are in anguish because they do
            not have the resources to care for their
            children adequately . . .

forgive us, and your church, our failure to resist the violence of poverty.

Lead us in resisting the assault on the poor, and comfort all women whose lives, or whose children's lives are stunted by lack of opportunity to grow with your strength and hope.

. . . when the baby is born, she forgets her suffering because she is happy that a baby has been born into the world. (John 16.21 GNB)

In many countries, the veil is worn as a symbol of dedicated lives, as a reminder of God's peace and God's justice. But it is not always so.

Wounded God, you took defenceless flesh and died on a cross.

We pray for: women who are casualties of war and the
        arms trade . . .
        women who mourn the violent deaths of
        loved ones . . .
        women whose spirits are killed a little more
        every day . . .

forgive us, and your church, our failure to confront the forces of death, and our easy separation of spirit from flesh.

Lead us in accepting the cost of discipleship for the sake of the joy of risen life, and in seeing that it is not suffering that saves, but love. Inspire all women who know only despair and sadness with your peace and promise of new life.

Then the veil hanging in the temple was torn in two, from top to bottom. (Matthew 27.51 GNB adapted)

We will remain silent no longer; we will stand alongside our sisters and proclaim Christ's call to us.

We will not cling to what is known; but together we will find new ways of sharing and living our faith.

We will not mourn at an empty tomb; but will share fullness of life of the risen Christ, who names us his apostles, and beloved daughters of God.

Amen.

These prayers were first written for the opening worship at a World Council of Churches/Conference of European Churches consultation on Violence Against Women, held at Corrymeela, Northern Ireland, in December 1994.

As each section of prayer was completed, women laid flowers on a white veil in the centre of the circle, in the Croi (Gaelic for 'heart'), the Corrymeela Community's worship building.

The closing lines are taken from the liturgy: Out of the Shadows, Women Overcoming Violence, held to mark the mid-point of the Ecumenical Decade of the Churches in Solidarity with Women, Manchester Cathedral, October 1993.

See, know, love: The different way

Do you see me?
As I really am,
not as the world sees me.
Flawed and faltering, yes,
but full of possibilities.
Hurt, even hateful sometimes,
but I also have my hopes.
I so much want someone to really see me.

God of grace and clarity,
we pray for people who are overlooked, unnoticed, even
hidden away by policy
in the corners of our minds, in the corners of our society:

> *beggars who embarrass us with their shamelessness and*
> *homelessness*
> *crazy people, confronting us with our own better-*
> *disguised chaos*
> *people whose illnesses arouse our deepest fears of blood*
> *and mortality*
> *people battered by the abuse of power, reminding us of*
> *our complicity with violence.*

We pray for your grace and clarity among us and within us.

And we bless you,
and give thanks for the people

> who look us in the eye
> who do not flinch at our humanity
> who do not turn away from our vulnerability
> who really see us with the eyes of love
> that different way of seeing.

Do you know me?
Or do you just know *about* me
about her,
about them,
and think you know it all?

God of truth and justice,
we pray for people who suffer the indignity of ignorance
whose lives are stunted by the prejudice of others
whose responsibility is restricted by 'we know what's best
*   for you':*

> *poor people*
> *single parents*
> *minorities*
> *gay people*
> *unemployed people*
> *people with handicaps*
> *people who don't fit our stereotypes.*

We pray for the humility to be attentive to truth
and for the courage to demand and stand firm for justice.

And we bless you,
and give thanks for the people

> who listen to us
> who walk beside us
> who measure their steps to ours
> long enough to know us with the knowledge of the heart
> that different way of knowing.

Do you love me?
Really love me?
Or is it just words?
Show me that you love me.

God of power and love,
we pray for people who suffer the death of love
and for those who have never known its quickening:

> bereft by death or abandonment
> stricken by cruelty or war
> frozen with fear
> hardened by the grindings of life and the indifference
>   of their kind
> children, women, men, in every continent and condition.

We pray for spirit to sing to the dry bones,
trusting your power to inspire new life,
even in the valley of the shadow of death.
And we pray for your love to lead us in the ways of care
so that our love may be given flesh, and not just dry words.

And we bless you,
and give thanks for the redeemed life of the world

> breathing, struggling, suffering
> embracing, demanding, holy
> that makes lovers of us
> lovers of each other
> lovers of life
> lovers of you
> our nearest, dearest desire,
> that different way of loving.

A psalm of love and anger

Oh my heart's heart, in love and anger I will turn to you,
for my soul cries out, 'Where is justice,
when will the balance be redressed
for the fearful dreams of children who sleep with knives,
for the beaten women, and the shamed and helpless men?'
Where is justice?
For the agony of hunger is not to be set
against the insatiable appetites of jaded palates.

In the villages and camps, the children lie bleeding,
and great wounds gape in their throats and sides.
In the city, there is no safety for them;
as the leaves blow through the night streets,
they are swept away, they disappear without trace
as if they had never been.

In the marketplace, weapons are bought and sold;
they change hands as easily as onions from a
       market-woman,
and killing comes lightly everywhere.
The value of people is weighed out on crooked scales
and found wanting,
they are discarded like bruised apples
because they lack the appearance of perfection.

But you, my heart's heart, you are careful;
like a thrifty housewife, who sees no waste in anything,
you gather up that which has been cast aside,
knowing its sweetness,
and take it home with you.

And I will see you in the camps and villages,
working late into the night,
showing patience in the midst of confusion,
reweaving the web of life.

I will see you in the cities,
seated in a circle, making new plans,
drawing attention,
naming the forgotten names.

I will see you in the marketplace,
dressed in black,
with the carved face of an old woman saying 'no' to war,
and you will stand your ground,
and you will seem beautiful to me.

For you are my sanctuary and my light,
my firm ground when the earth cracks
under the weight of warring gods.
As a woman in mortal danger flees to her sisters
and finds refuge,
so you will comfort me, and dress my wounds with
    tenderness.
And when the flame of courage burns low in me,
your breath, as gentle as a sleeping child,
will stir the ashes of my heart.

Teach me to know your judgement as my friend,
that I may never be ashamed of justice,
or so proud that I flee from mercy.
For your love is never less than justice,
and your strength is tenderness.
You contain my soul's yearning,
and in your encompassing, I am free.